SCHOLASTIC

180 ESSENTIAL VOCABULARY WORDS FOR 5TH GRADE

Independent Learning Packets That Help Students Learn the Most Important Words They Need to Succeed in School

Linda Ward Beech

NEW YORK • TORONTO • LONDON • AUCKLAND • SYDNEY
MEXICO CITY • NEW DELHI • HONG KONG • BUENOS AIRES

Teaching *Resources*

Editor: Mela Ottaiano
Cover design: Brian LaRossa
Interior design: Melinda Belter
Interior illustrations: Mike Moran

ISBN-13: 978-0-439-89736-5
ISBN-10: 0-439-89736-X

1 2 3 4 5 6 7 8 9 10   40   15 14 13 12 11 10 09

TABLE OF CONTENTS

Introduction

Academic vocabulary refers to words that are commonly found in textbooks and used in assignments, content area standards, and standardized tests. Just as specialized words are used in fields such as journalism, medicine, and law enforcement, academic vocabulary is the language of the classroom, school, and educational process. Recognizing these words and comprehending what they mean is, therefore, crucial to a student's academic success. The purpose of this book is to help students become familiar with the academic vocabulary most often used at their grade level. In this way, they will be better prepared to understand and successfully complete classroom work, homework assignments, and tests.

The lessons in this book are organized around curriculum areas and other common school topics. Each four-page lesson introduces ten words and provides various ways for students to explore their meaning and usage.

Materials

As you introduce the lessons, be sure to have the following items available:

Dictionaries
Thesauruses
Writing tools or computers
Student portfolios of written work

Tips for Using the Lessons

- Make a practice of using the lesson words often in classroom discussions and assignments. Call attention to these words as they come up.

- Consider having students make a set of word cards for each lesson. You might also make a class set and place it in your language arts center.

- Many words have more than one meaning, including some that are not given in the lesson. Point out additional meanings or invite students to discover and share them.

- Review parts of speech with students before each lesson. Many words can be used as more than one part of speech, including examples that are not given in this book. Encourage students to monitor their use of these words.

- Be sure to have students complete the Portfolio Page assignments on the second page of each lesson. Add your own writing assignments as well. Applying the lesson words in independent writing activities is essential in making the words part of students' vocabulary.

- Encourage students to consult more than one reference and to compare information.

 **TEXT MESSAGE** You'll find a complete alphabetized list of all the lesson words in the Word List at the back of the book. Each page number listed identifies the first page of the lesson in which the word is found.

Lesson Organization

Each lesson is four pages long and introduces ten academic words.

The first lesson page includes:

lesson words

statement of lesson focus

simple sentences explaining meaning of words

cloze exercise *

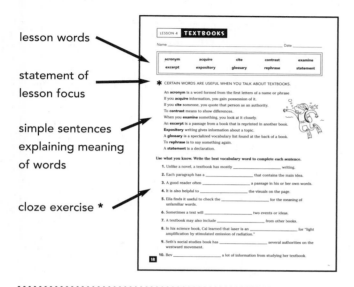

The second page includes:

lesson words

one or more exercises focusing on meaning

Portfolio Page writing assignment

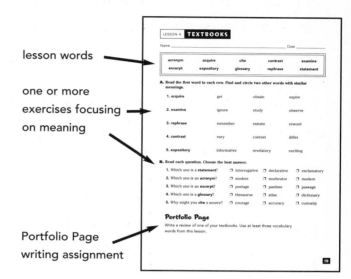

> * **ALERT STUDENTS TO LOOK AT THE SUBJECTS OF THE CLOZE SENTENCES** to determine if they are singular or plural because that will affect the form of the verbs they use. Students should also use the correct verb tense in these sentences. For nouns, students should determine whether they need to use the singular or plural form.

The third page includes:

lesson words

two or three exercises focusing on suffixes, prefixes, other meanings, parts of speech, word roots, or word structure

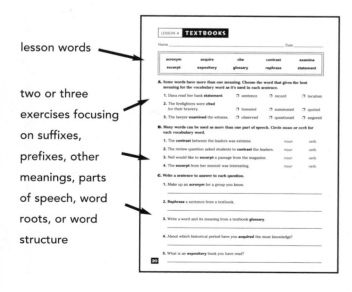

The fourth page includes:

a puzzle, game, maze, or other learning activity using the words

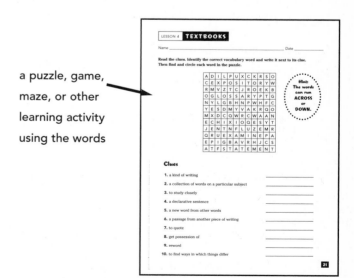

SCHOOL

Name _____ Date _____

discipline	enroll	essential	information	integrate
intermediate	promote	section	supervise	translation

✱ SOME WORDS ARE USEFUL TO KNOW BECAUSE THEY REFER TO SCHOOL.

Discipline is controlled behavior resulting from training.

If you sign up to take a class, you **enroll** in it.

Something **essential** is of the greatest importance.

If you have facts about a topic, you have **information**.

When you combine things into a whole, you **integrate** them.

Intermediate means "in-between."

If you **promote** something, you advance it.

A **section** is a part of a whole.

When you **supervise** something, you direct the action of it.

A **translation** is something that is expressed in another language.

Use what you know. Write the best vocabulary word to complete each sentence.

1. Last year, Zack was a beginner, but this year he is in the _____ group.

2. Reading is an _____ skill.

3. Holly plans to _____ in Mr. Fine's art class.

4. The book you have chosen is a _____ of the Spanish version.

5. Our school is divided into four _____ of students.

6. It takes _____ to do your homework as soon as you get home from school.

7. Ana found _____ about Peru on the Internet.

8. In her discussion, Ms. Vega tried to _____ history and literature.

9. Which teacher will _____ this after-school program?

10. At the end of the year the principal will _____ us to the next grade.

180 Essential Vocabulary Words for 5th Grade © 2009 by Linda Ward Beech, Scholastic Teaching Resources

Name _____ Date _____

| discipline | enroll | essential | information | integrate |
| intermediate | promote | section | supervise | translation |

A. Read the first word in each row. Find and circle two other words in that row with similar meanings.

1. enroll	enlist	register	exit	exercise
2. essential	aromatic	fundamental	excellent	indispensable
3. section	entire	part	portion	second
4. supervise	control	superheat	serve	oversee
5. integrate	interfere	unify	intercept	consolidate
6. information	memory	data	knowledge	inflection
7. promote	progress	irritate	advance	promise

B. Read each question. Choose the best answer.

1. Which one is **intermediate**?   ❏ beginning   ❏ middle   ❏ final
2. What does a **translation** do?   ❏ depress   ❏ repress   ❏ express
3. Which one is **discipline**?   ❏ forgetting   ❏ training   ❏ hoping

Portfolio Page

Write an e-mail giving advice to someone who will be a newcomer at your school. Use at least three vocabulary words from this lesson.

SCHOOL

Name _____ Date _____

| discipline | enroll | essential | information | integrate |
| intermediate | promote | section | supervise | translation |

A. The lesson words below have suffixes. A suffix is added to the end of a word to change its meaning and often its part of speech. Underline the suffix in each word. Then, write a sentence using the word. Use a dictionary if needed.

1. supervision _____

2. translator _____

3. intermediary _____

4. enrollment _____

5. integration _____

B. Write a sentence to answer each question.

1. What is a cause that you would **promote**?

_____

2. Why is education considered **essential**?

_____

3. In what **section** of the library would you find the life story of Thomas Jefferson?

_____

4. What **information** would you need to mail a package?

_____

5. How could **discipline** help you improve your grades?

_____

180 Essential Vocabulary Words for 5th Grade © 2009 by Linda Ward Beech, Scholastic Teaching Resources

Name _____ Date _____

Play the Word Clue Game.

Write the best vocabulary word for each clue. Use each word only once.

Clues	Vocabulary Words
1. Is the opposite of *unimportant*	
2. Has the word *media* in it	
3. Is a synonym for *segment*	
4. Comes from the Latin word *discipulus*, meaning "student"	
5. Related to *promotion, promoter*	
6. Can mean "knowledge"	
7. Begins with a prefix that means "across"	
8. Is an antonym of *segregate*	
9. Comes from Latin words *super*, meaning "over" and *videre*, meaning "to see"	
10. Rhymes with *patrol*	

Name _____ Date _____

analogy	**classic**	**diction**	**figurative**	**foreshadow**
infer	**insight**	**introduction**	**motive**	**narrative**

✳ YOU USE CERTAIN WORDS WHEN YOU TALK ABOUT READING.

An **analogy** is a statement in which the relationship of one thing is likened to that of another thing.

A **classic** is an author or work thought to be of the highest rank.

The choice and use of words in speaking or writing is called **diction**.

Figurative language includes figures of speech such as similes.

An author may **foreshadow** an event by giving a hint in advance.

When you **infer** something, you make a conclusion based on evidence.

Insight is the ability to see the nature of something.

An **introduction** is a section at the beginning of a book that prepares the way for what follows.

A **motive** is a reason for doing something.

A **narrative** is a story.

Use what you know. Write the best vocabulary word to complete each sentence.

1. The plays of Shakespeare are considered _____ .

2. Poetry often contains _____ language.

3. The character's _____ was not yet clear to Jade.

4. As Lamont read the book, he gained _____ into the character's behavior.

5. The _____ compared two sets of synonyms.

6. The _____ explained what the reader would learn.

7. Colin likes to read a _____ text with a good plot.

8. The author's vocabulary and _____ made the description vivid.

9. What can you _____ from this paragraph about the accident?

10. The author _____ this event earlier in the story.

180 Essential Vocabulary Words for 5th Grade © 2009 by Linda Ward Beech, Scholastic Teaching Resources

Name _____ Date _____

analogy	classic	diction	figurative	foreshadow
infer	insight	introduction	motive	narrative

A. Read each pair of words. Write a vocabulary word that has the same or almost the same meaning.

1. phraseology, wording _____

2. foretell, hint _____

3. deduce, conclude _____

4. intuition, perception _____

5. preface, foreword _____

6. purpose, explanation _____

B. Read each question. Choose the best answer.

1. Which one is **classic**? ❏ past ❏ present ❏ future

2. Which one describes **figurative**? ❏ fanciful ❏ typical ❏ local

3. Which one is key to an **analogy**? ❏ similarity ❏ simulation ❏ simplicity

4. Which one is a **narrative**? ❏ textbook ❏ storybook ❏ cookbook

Portfolio Page

Write a brief profile of a favorite book character. Use at least three vocabulary words from this lesson.

Name _____ Date _____

| analogy | classic | diction | figurative | foreshadow |
| infer | insight | introduction | motive | narrative |

A. Read the word meaning in each sentence. Then, write the vocabulary word that comes from the Greek or Latin word.

1. The Greek word *analogos* means "resembling." _____

2. The Latin word *dicere* means "to say." _____

3. The Latin word *inferre* means "to bring in." _____

4. The Old English word *sihth* means "vision or thing seen." _____

B. Write a vocabulary word that is an antonym of each word below.

1. literal _____

2. epilogue _____

C. Write a sentence to answer each question.

1. What **classic** have you read or would like to read?

_____

2. Why might an author **foreshadow** a story event?

_____

3. What is a key **motive** for many of Harry Potter's actions?

_____

4. What is the main setting of your favorite **narrative**?

_____

180 Essential Vocabulary Words for 5th Grade © 2009 by Linda Ward Beech, Scholastic Teaching Resources

Name _____ Date _____

Read the clues. Complete the puzzle using the vocabulary words from this lesson.

1. a narrated account

2. why a character acts a certain way

3. *Gulliver's Travels* is an example.

4. a use of vocabulary

5. what a reader does to increase understanding of a text

6. An example is: *Bright* is to *dim* as *nice* is to *mean*.

7. It comes at the beginning.

8. to give a preview

9. A metaphor is an example of this kind of language.

10. wisdom and understanding about something

1. __ __ __ **R** __ __ __ __ __

2. __ __ __ __ __ **E**

3. __ __ **A** __ __ __ __

4. **D** __ __ __ __ __ __

5. __ __ **F** __ __

6. __ __ __ __ **O** __ __

7. __ __ __ **R** __ __ __ __ __ __ __ __

8. **F** __ __ __ __ __ __ __ __ __ __

9. __ __ __ **U** __ __ __ __ __ __

10. __ **N** __ __ __ __ __

WRITING

Name _____ Date _____

| abbreviation | clarify | composition | compound | convince |
| header | inspiration | modify | revision | specific |

✱ YOU USE CERTAIN WORDS WHEN YOU TALK ABOUT WRITING.

In an **abbreviation**, part of a word stands for the whole word.

If you **clarify** something, you make it clear.

A **composition** is a short essay.

A **compound** is something that has more than one part.

If you **convince** someone, you win that person over.

A **header** is information that runs along the top of a page of text.

Inspiration is an influence that results in a good idea.

Some words **modify** or limit the meaning of other words.

A **revision** is a corrected or improved form of writing.

Specific means "particular."

> Mr.
> AND
> *Mrs.*

Use what you know. Write the best vocabulary word to complete each sentence.

1. The editorial tries to _____ readers to vote for this candidate.

2. Amber needed some _____ before she could write a poem.

3. Use the _____ for "street" on the address.

4. A _____ sentence has two independent clauses.

5. Miss Reyes assigned a _____ for English homework.

6. Trish forgot to put a _____ at the top of her first draft.

7. An adjective _____ a noun.

8. Jason's _____ was an improvement over his first draft.

9. The teacher asked Blake to _____ her statement.

10. Try to use _____ verbs to make your writing more interesting.

180 Essential Vocabulary Words for 5th Grade © 2009 by Linda Ward Beech, Scholastic Teaching Resources

Name _____ Date _____

abbreviation	clarify	composition	compound	convince
header	inspiration	modify	revision	specific

A. Draw a line from each vocabulary word to match it with a synonym.

1. convince   **a.** motivation

2. composition   **b.** abridgment

3. specific   **c.** correction

4. abbreviation   **d.** essay

5. modify   **e.** persuade

6. revision   **f.** limit

7. inspiration   **g.** precise

B. Read each question. Choose the best answer.

1. Where is a **header**?   ❑ bottom   ❑ middle   ❑ top

2. Which one is a **compound** word?   ❑ classroom   ❑ class   ❑ classify

3. What do you **clarify**?   ❑ seeking   ❑ hearing   ❑ meaning

Portfolio Page

Write three compound sentences. Use at least three vocabulary words
from this lesson.

Name _____ Date _____

| abbreviation | clarify | composition | compound | convince |
| header | inspiration | modify | revision | specific |

A. For each number, read the three words. Shade the word in one of the bottom boxes that is an antonym of the word in the top box.

1. convince

| dissuade | sway |

2. header

| title | footer |

3. clarify

| confuse | explain |

4. specific

| vague | definite |

5. compound

| multiple | simple |

6. modify

| preserve | alter |

B. The vocabulary words below contain a suffix. Write the base word for each one. Then, use the base word in a sentence.

1. inspiration   _____

_____

2. abbreviation   _____

_____

3. revision   _____

_____

4. composition   _____

_____

180 Essential Vocabulary Words for 5th Grade © 2009 by Linda Ward Beech, Scholastic Teaching Resources

Name _____ Date _____

Read each clue. Write the correct vocabulary word in the spaces below. Then, write the letters from the shaded boxes in order on the lines to find the mystery word.

1. shed some light on something ▢▢▢▢▢▢▢

2. an improved piece of writing ▢▢▢▢▢▢▢

3. something you might write in school ▢▢▢▢▢▢▢▢▢▢

4. what adverbs do to verbs ▢▢▢▢▢▢

5. a kind of sentence you might use in writing ▢▢▢▢▢▢▢▢

6. what a persuasive paragraph tries to do ▢▢▢▢▢▢▢▢

7. a shortening of a word ▢▢▢▢▢▢▢▢▢▢▢

8. the opposite of general ▢▢▢▢▢▢▢▢

9. information at the top of a page ▢▢▢▢▢▢

10. a brilliant idea ▢▢▢▢▢▢▢▢▢▢

Mystery Word

Writing is an important way to __ __ __ __ __ __ __ __ __ __ __ __ _e_ .

180 Essential Vocabulary Words for 5th Grade © 2009 by Linda Ward Beech, Scholastic Teaching Resources

TEXTBOOKS

Name _____ Date _____

acquire	**acronym**	**cite**	**contrast**	**examine**
excerpt	**expository**	**glossary**	**rephrase**	**statement**

✻ CERTAIN WORDS ARE USEFUL WHEN YOU TALK ABOUT TEXTBOOKS.

If you **acquire** information, you gain possession of it.

An **acronym** is a word formed from the first letters of a name or phrase.

If you **cite** someone, you quote that person as an authority.

To **contrast** means "to show differences."

When you **examine** something, you look at it closely.

An **excerpt** is a passage from a book that is reprinted in another book.

Expository writing gives information about a topic.

A **glossary** is a specialized vocabulary list found at the back of a book.

To **rephrase** is to say something again.

A **statement** is a declaration.

Use what you know. Write the best vocabulary word to complete each sentence.

1. Unlike a novel, a textbook has mostly _____ writing.

2. Each paragraph has a _____ that contains the main idea.

3. A good reader often _____ a passage in his or her own words.

4. It is also helpful to _____ the visuals on the page.

5. Ella finds it useful to check the _____ for the meaning of unfamiliar words.

6. Sometimes a text will _____ two events or ideas.

7. A textbook may also include _____ from other books.

8. In his science book, Cal learned that laser is an _____ for "light amplification by stimulated emission of radiation."

9. Seth's social studies book has _____ several authorities on the westward movement.

10. Bev _____ a lot of information from studying her textbook.

180 Essential Vocabulary Words for 5th Grade © 2009 by Linda Ward Beech, Scholastic Teaching Resources

Name _____ Date _____

acquire	acronym	cite	contrast	examine
excerpt	expository	glossary	rephrase	statement

A. Read the first word in each row. Find and circle two other words with similar meanings.

1. acquire   get   obtain   expire

2. examine   ignore   study   observe

3. rephrase   remember   restate   reword

4. contrast   vary   contest   differ

5. expository   informative   revelatory   exciting

B. Read each question. Choose the best answer.

1. Which one is a **statement**?   ❏ interrogative   ❏ declarative   ❏ exclamatory

2. Which one is an **acronym**?   ❏ modem   ❏ moderator   ❏ modern

3. Which one is an **excerpt**?   ❏ postage   ❏ pastime   ❏ passage

4. Which one is a **glossary**?   ❏ thesaurus   ❏ atlas   ❏ dictionary

5. Why might you **cite** a source?   ❏ courage   ❏ accuracy   ❏ curiosity

Portfolio Page

Write a review of one of your textbooks. Use at least three vocabulary words from this lesson.

180 Essential Vocabulary Words for 5th Grade © 2009 by Linda Ward Beech, Scholastic Teaching Resources

TEXTBOOKS

Name _____ Date _____

| acquire | acronym | cite | contrast | examine |
| excerpt | expository | glossary | rephrase | statement |

A. **Some words have more than one meaning. Choose the word that gives the best meaning for the vocabulary word as it's used in each sentence.**

1. Dana read her bank **statement**.　❒ sentence　❒ record　❒ location

2. The firefighters were **cited** for their bravery.　❒ honored　❒ summoned　❒ quoted

3. The lawyer **examined** the witness.　❒ observed　❒ questioned　❒ angered

B. **Many words can be used as more than one part of speech. Circle *noun* or *verb* for each vocabulary word.**

1. The **contrast** between the leaders was extreme.　　noun　　verb

2. The review question asked students to **contrast** the leaders.　　noun　　verb

3. Neil would like to **excerpt** a passage from the magazine.　　noun　　verb

4. The **excerpt** from her memoir was interesting.　　noun　　verb

C. **Write a sentence to respond items 1–5 below.**

1. Make up an **acronym** for a group you know.

_____

2. **Rephrase** a sentence from a textbook.

_____

3. Write a word and its meaning from a textbook **glossary**.

_____

4. About which historical period have you **acquired** the most knowledge?

_____

5. What is an **expository** book you have read?

_____

180 Essential Vocabulary Words for 5th Grade © 2009 by Linda Ward Beech, Scholastic Teaching Resources

TEXTBOOKS

Name _____ Date _____

Read the clues. Identify the correct vocabulary word and write it next to its clue.
Then, find and circle each word in the puzzle.

A	D	I	L	P	U	X	C	K	R	S	O
C	E	X	P	O	S	I	T	O	R	Y	W
R	M	V	Z	T	C	J	R	O	E	K	B
O	G	L	O	S	S	A	R	Y	P	T	G
N	Y	L	G	B	H	N	P	W	H	F	C
Y	E	S	D	M	Y	V	A	K	R	Q	O
M	X	D	C	Q	W	R	C	W	A	A	N
E	C	H	I	X	I	O	Q	E	S	Y	T
J	E	N	T	N	F	L	U	Z	E	M	R
Q	R	U	E	X	A	M	I	N	E	P	A
E	P	I	G	B	A	V	R	H	J	C	S
A	T	F	S	T	A	T	E	M	E	N	T

Hint:
The words
can run
ACROSS
or
DOWN.

Clues

1. a kind of writing   _____

2. a collection of words on a particular subject   _____

3. to study closely   _____

4. a declarative sentence   _____

5. a new word from other words   _____

6. a passage from another piece of writing   _____

7. to quote   _____

8. get possession of   _____

9. reword   _____

10. to find ways in which things differ   _____

Name _____ Date _____

asset	compute	credit	finance	fund
income	inventory	invest	minimum	scarce

✱ YOU USE CERTAIN WORDS WHEN YOU TALK ABOUT ECONOMICS.

An **asset** is a valuable possession.

If you **compute** a math problem, you figure it out.

Credit is someone's ability to meet debts.

Finance is the management of money.

A **fund** is money set aside for certain purposes.

Income means "earnings."

An **inventory** is a list of possessions or goods.

When you **invest**, you use money to make a profit.

A **minimum** is the least amount.

If something is **scarce**, there is little of it.

Use what you know. Write the best vocabulary word to complete each sentence.

1. The class set up a _____ for the spring field trip.

2. Because of the drought, some vegetables were _____ this year.

3. Mr. Lake's house is his biggest _____ .

4. Mrs. Watkins had good _____ because she paid her bills on time.

5. The students _____ how much money they needed for refreshments.

6. Ms. Chang made an _____ of the goods in her store.

7. Dad decided to _____ in a new company.

8. Blair has a new job and now brings home a good _____ .

9. The charity asked each person to give a _____ of one dollar to the cause.

10. Jerry wanted to read books about _____ so he could manage his allowance wisely.

180 Essential Vocabulary Words for 5th Grade © 2009 by Linda Ward Beech, Scholastic Teaching Resources

MATH/ECONOMICS

Name _____ Date _____

| asset | compute | credit | finance | fund |
| income | inventory | invest | minimum | scarce |

A. Read each pair of words. Write a vocabulary word that has the same or almost the same meaning.

1. lacking, insufficient _____

2. calculate, reckon _____

3. belongings, property _____

4. least, smallest _____

5. revenue, wages _____

6. list, record _____

B. Read each question. Choose the best answer.

1. Why do you **invest**?   ❑ to borrow   ❑ to pay   ❑ to gain

2. What can you do with **credit**?   ❑ charge   ❑ change   ❑ barter

3. What is a **fund**?   ❑ spending   ❑ savings   ❑ losing

4. What is **finance** about?   ❑ affection   ❑ duty   ❑ money

Portfolio Page

Write a list of questions about managing money. Use at least three vocabulary words from this lesson.

180 Essential Vocabulary Words for 5th Grade © 2009 by Linda Ward Beech, Scholastic Teaching Resources

Name _____ Date _____

| asset | compute | credit | finance | fund |
| income | inventory | invest | minimum | scarce |

A. Read each set of words. Underline the two words that are antonyms. Use a dictionary if needed.

1.
minute

maximum

minimum

2.
debit

orbit

credit

3.
plentiful

scarce

scary

4.
expenses

interest

income

5.
insult

invest

divest

6.
liability

asset

assert

B. Some words have more than one meaning. Choose the word or phrase that gives the best meaning for the vocabulary word as it's used in each sentence.

1. She has a **fund** of knowledge about birds. ❑ supply ❑ savings ❑ lack

2. My parents will **finance** the trip. ❑ end ❑ pay for ❑ manage

C. Underline the best ending for each sentence.

1. An **inventory** helps a store _____ .

    a. advertise goods   **b.** display goods   **c.** restock goods

2. In a restaurant, you might **compute** in order to _____ .

    a. choose a dessert   **b.** determine a tip   **c.** meet a friend

MATH/ECONOMICS

Name _____ Date _____

Read the clues. Then, complete the puzzle using the vocabulary words from this lesson.

Across

2. money collected for a particular use
6. a record of items stocked by a store
7. money that someone earns for work
8. the management of money
10. calculate

Down

1. use money to gain interest or profit
3. opposite of maximum
4. confidence in a buyer's ability to pay
5. not readily available
9. something you own that represents wealth

SOCIAL STUDIES

Name _____ Date _____

elevation	employ	establish	innocent	issue
military	profession	property	survey	transfer

✳ YOU USE CERTAIN WORDS WHEN YOU TALK ABOUT SOCIAL STUDIES.

Elevation is the height of land above sea level.

If you **employ** someone, you provide that person with work.

When you **establish** something, you set it up.

Innocent means "not guilty."

An **issue** is a subject under discussion.

Military refers to the armed forces.

A **profession** is an occupation.

Property is something that you own.

A **survey** is a study done about something.

If you **transfer** something, you move it from one place to another.

Use what you know. Write the best vocabulary word to complete each sentence.

1. The jury found the defendant _____ of the crime.

2. The soldiers lived on a _____ base.

3. The _____ of the mountain was more than 12,000 feet.

4. Jared _____ his wallet from one pocket to the other.

5. Our town was _____ in 1809.

6. The gardener plans to _____ three more people for the summer.

7. We answered questions on the _____ about our neighborhood.

8. One of the _____ they discussed was pollution.

9. There is a fence at the edge of their _____ .

10. Someday, Penny hopes to go into the medical _____ .

180 Essential Vocabulary Words for 5th Grade © 2009 by Linda Ward Beech, Scholastic Teaching Resources

SOCIAL STUDIES

Name _____ Date _____

| elevation | employ | establish | innocent | issue |
| military | profession | property | survey | transfer |

A. For each word below, write the vocabulary word that is a synonym.

1. height _____

2. vocation _____

3. start _____

B. Read the vocabulary word. Underline the word that is a synonym. Circle the word that is an antonym.

1. employ   fire   help   hire

2. innocent   innovative   blameless   guilty

3. transfer   move   remain   translate

C. Read each question. Choose the best answer.

1. Which one refers to **property**?

❏ you're   ❏ yours   ❏ you'll

2. Which one is a **survey**?

❏ building   ❏ magazine   ❏ questionnaire

3. Which one is **military**?

❏ literature   ❏ insect   ❏ armament

4. Which one is often an election **issue**?

❏ taxes   ❏ stamps   ❏ voters

Portfolio Page

Imagine that you are a newspaper editor. Write three headlines for stories in the news. Use at least three vocabulary words from this lesson.

SOCIAL STUDIES

Name _____ Date _____

elevation	employ	establish	innocent	issue
military	profession	property	survey	transfer

A. Some words have more than one meaning. Choose the word or phrase that gives the best meaning for the vocabulary word as it's used in each sentence.

1. Mom **established** the date of the party.
❏ founded   ❏ confirmed   ❏ asked

2. The swimmer will **employ** all her strength in this race.
❏ use   ❏ hire   ❏ ignore

3. Dad **surveyed** the messy room.
❏ cleaned   ❏ questioned   ❏ looked over

4. What is the main **property** of a diamond?
❏ yard   ❏ belonging   ❏ characteristic

5. She had the chance for **elevation** at her job.
❏ advancement   ❏ height   ❏ elevator

6. The post office will **issue** new stamps.
❏ topic   ❏ recall   ❏ make available

B. Write a sentence to answer each question.

1. What **profession** do you hope to have someday?

_____

2. Why might it be hard to **transfer** to another school?

_____

C. Many words can be used as more than one part of speech. Write *noun* or *adjective* for each vocabulary word.

1. The little girl was such an **innocent**. _____

2. Was the man **innocent** or guilty? _____

3. The **military** uniform looked good on the cadet. _____

4. The **military** has a large budget. _____

180 Essential Vocabulary Words for 5th Grade © 2009 by Linda Ward Beech, Scholastic Teaching Resources

Name _____ Date _____

Play the So Is Game.

Complete each sentence with a vocabulary word from this lesson.

1. The army is part of the _____ and so is the navy.

2. Mt. Everest has a high _____ and so does Mt. Kilimanjaro.

3. *Shift* means "move" and so does _____ .

4. Global warming is an _____ of public concern and so are endangered animals.

5. The law is a _____ and so is teaching.

6. Companies _____ many people and so does the government.

7. *Create* means "to originate" and so does _____ .

8. A poll collects information and so does a _____ .

9. *Guiltless* means _____ and so does *faultless*.

10. A car is someone's _____ and so is a house.

Name _____ Date _____

amendment	consent	democracy	diverse	executive
guarantee	judicial	legislative	minority	policy

✱ YOU USE CERTAIN WORDS WHEN TALKING ABOUT GOVERNMENT.

An **amendment** is a change for the better.

If you **consent** to something, you agree to it.

A **democracy** is a form of government in which power belongs to the people.

Diverse means "varied."

The **executive** branch of government puts the laws in effect.

A **guarantee** is a promise.

The **judicial** branch of government decides what laws mean.

The **legislative** branch of government makes the laws.

A **minority** is a group numbering less than half of the total.

A **policy** is a course of action that a government takes.

Use what you know. Write the best vocabulary word to complete each sentence.

1. The political system of the United States is a _____ .

2. Our Constitution _____ us certain rights.

3. The president is head of the _____ branch.

4. The Supreme Court is part of the _____ branch.

5. Congress makes up the _____ branch.

6. We can change the Constitution by passing an _____ .

7. The government rules by the _____ of the people.

8. The government forms _____ for dealing with other nations.

9. If a group is a _____ , it still has the same rights as others.

10. Because people have come from so many places, the population is

_____ .

180 Essential Vocabulary Words for 5th Grade © 2009 by Linda Ward Beech, Scholastic Teaching Resources

Name _____ Date _____

amendment	consent	democracy	diverse	executive
guarantee	judicial	legislative	minority	policy

A. Read each question. Choose the best answer.

1. Which one is an **executive**? ❏ shopper ❏ artist ❏ president

2. Which one is a **minority**? ❏ most ❏ few ❏ all

3. Which one is in a **democracy**? ❏ emperor ❏ czar ❏ representative

4. Which one is in a **legislative** body? ❏ lawmaker ❏ lawbreaker ❏ legacy

5. Which one is **judicial**? ❏ teacher ❏ judge ❏ senator

B. Read the vocabulary word. Find and circle two other words in that row with similar meanings.

1. **consent**	convict	assent	concur	content
2. **diverse**	different	dissimilar	divided	divine
3. **amendment**	ambush	revision	accident	improvement
4. **policy**	police	program	pocket	strategy
5. **guarantee**	pledge	guard	assurance	law

Portfolio Page

Write a paragraph about one way in which government affects your life. Use at least three vocabulary words from this lesson.

Name _____ Date _____

amendment	consent	democracy	diverse	executive
guarantee	judicial	legislative	minority	policy

A. For each word below, write the vocabulary word that is an antonym.

1. majority _____

2. homogenous _____

3. dissent _____

4. renege _____

B. Write a vocabulary word that is related to each word below. Then, write another word that is related to both words. Use related words you already know or find words in a resource.

Word	Related Vocabulary Word	Another Related Word
1. politician	_____	_____
2. judicious	_____	_____
3. execute	_____	_____
4. amends	_____	_____
5. democratic	_____	_____
6. legislate	_____	_____

180 Essential Vocabulary Words for 5th Grade © 2009 by Linda Ward Beech, Scholastic Teaching Resources

Name _____ Date _____

Play the Word Clue Game.

Write the best vocabulary word for each clue. Use each word only once.

Clues	Vocabulary Words
1. comes from the Greek word *polis* meaning "city"	
2. the branch of government in which a senator works	
3. means the same as *accede*	
4. describes the U.S. government	
5. the chief officer of a government	
6. rhymes with *warranty*	
7. can also mean "a period of being under a legal age"	
8. comes from the Latin word *judex* meaning "judge"	
9. is related to *diversity* and *diversify*	
10. The first 10 of these are called the Bill of Rights.	

Name _____ Date _____

| body | convert | distinct | elements | erosion |
| evolve | formula | function | medical | technical |

✱ YOU USE CERTAIN WORDS WHEN YOU TALK ABOUT SCIENCE.

A **body** is the whole of a person, plant, or animal.

To **convert** is to change something into another form.

Something that is **distinct** is separate.

All matter is composed of the known 103 **elements**.

Erosion is a gradual wearing away.

Evolve means "develop gradually."

A **formula** is a recipe for doing something.

The **function** of something is its role.

Medical refers to the science of medicine.

Technical refers to the industrial arts or applied sciences.

Use what you know. Write the best vocabulary to complete each sentence.

1. Heavy rains caused _____ on the hillsides.

2. The _____ of an insect differs from that of a mammal.

3. One of the _____ is oxygen, and another is hydrogen.

4. This flower has five _____ petals.

5. When there was a _____ emergency, we called an ambulance.

6. You can _____ alternating current into direct current.

7. Raki works as a _____ assistant at an engineering company.

8. The students learned that an elephant's trunk has more than one

_____ .

9. The scientist follows a _____ to mix these chemicals.

10. Some parts of this plant have _____ over time.

Name _____ Date _____

| body | convert | distinct | elements | erosion |
| evolve | formula | function | medical | technical |

A. Draw a line from each vocabulary word to match it with a synonym.

1. **medical**   **a.** develop

2. **convert**   **b.** recipe

3. **evolve**   **c.** transform

4. **distinct**   **d.** healing

5. **formula**   **e.** purpose

6. **function**   **f.** clear

B. Read each sentence. Choose the best answer.

1. Which one is an **element**?   ❐ gold   ❐ golf   ❐ goat

2. What causes **erosion**?   ❐ moon   ❐ cloud   ❐ wind

3. Which one is **technical**?   ❐ oral   ❐ digital   ❐ annual

4. Which has a **body**?   ❐ category ❐ bobcat   ❐ catsup

Portfolio Page

Write the introduction to a science fiction story. Use at least three vocabulary words from this lesson.

180 Essential Vocabulary Words for 5th Grade © 2009 by Linda Ward Beech, Scholastic Teaching Resources

Name _____ Date _____

body	convert	distinct	elements	erosion
evolve	formula	function	medical	technical

A. Some words have more than one meaning. Choose the word that gives the best meaning for the vocabulary word as it's used in each sentence.

1. My parents went to a large **function**. ❏ purpose   ❏ event   ❏ building

2. The boys grew more excited as their plan **evolved**. ❏ changed   ❏ backfired   ❏ unfolded

3. Mom gave the baby her **formula**. ❏ toy   ❏ mixture   ❏ plan

4. Helen was in her **element** as she played the piano. ❏ environment   ❏ compound   ❏ school

5. The poet has a large **body** of work. ❏ collection   ❏ part   ❏ box

B. For each word below, write a vocabulary word that is an antonym.

1. unclear _____

2. construction _____

C. Write a vocabulary word that is related to each pair of words below.

1. conversion, convertible _____

2. technicality, technician _____

3. medicinal, medication _____

180 Essential Vocabulary Words for 5th Grade © 2009 by Linda Ward Beech, Scholastic Teaching Resources

Name _____ Date _____

Read the clues. Complete the puzzle using the vocabulary words from this lesson.

1. comes from the Greek word *technikos* meaning "skill"

2. a definite plan or method

3. You feed, wash, and dress this everyday.

4. opposite of fuzzy

5. adjective describing professionals who work in a hospital

6. Caused by wind and rain

7. to change gradually over time

8. when you change fractions to decimals

9. job or role

10. Copper is an example.

1. **T** __ __ __ __ __ __ __ __

2. __ __ **R** __ __ __ __

3. __ __ __ **Y**

4. __ __ **S** __ __ __ __

5. __ __ __ __ __ **C** __ __

6. __ __ __ __ **I** __

7. **E** __ __ __ __ __

8. __ __ **N** __ __ __ __

9. __ __ __ **C** __ __ __

10. **E** __ __ __ __ __ __ __

SCIENCE/EXPERIMENTS

Name _____ Date _____

| assess | comparison | discovery | evident | investigation |
| precise | procedure | simulate | solution | valid |

✷ YOU USE CERTAIN WORDS WHEN YOU TALK ABOUT SCIENCE EXPERIMENTS.

When you **assess** a result, you examine it critically and estimate its merit.

In a **comparison**, you find likenesses and differences.

A **discovery** is something known for the first time.

When something is **evident**, it is easily seen.

An **investigation** is a careful search.

Precise means "exact."

A **procedure** is a way of doing things.

Simulate means "imitate."

A **solution** is the solving of a problem.

If an argument is **valid**, it is sound.

Use what you know. Write the best vocabulary word to complete each sentence.

1. Muriel made a _____ between two different leaves.

2. Cora's objections to the results were based on facts and therefore

   _____ .

3. It was _____ to the teacher that some students had made a mistake.

4. The students were expected to give _____ answers.

5. When Neva _____ her experiment, she felt she had done a good job.

6. Mr. Gomez wrote the _____ for students to follow on the board.

7. In his project, Phil tried to _____ the results of erosion on sand.

8. For their project, the students did an _____ of pollution.

9. Every scientist hopes to make a great _____ one day.

10. Lucy explained the _____ she arrived at in her experiment.

180 Essential Vocabulary Words for 5th Grade © 2009 by Linda Ward Beech, Scholastic Teaching Resources

Name _____ Date _____

assess	comparison	discovery	evident	investigation
precise	procedure	simulate	solution	valid

A. For each word below, write a vocabulary word that is a synonym.

1. evaluate _____

2. inquiry _____

3. pretend _____

B. Read the vocabulary word. Underline the word that is a synonym. Circle the word that is an antonym.

1. **precise**   preliminary   accurate   vague

2. **evident**   unclear   plain   eventual

3. **valid**   valuable   ineffective   true

4. **discovery**   loss   finding   distance

C. Read each question. Choose the best answer.

1. What is in a **comparison**?   ❏ differences   ❏ difficulties   ❏ disagreements

2. Which one is a **procedure**?   ❏ guess   ❏ plan   ❏ rehearsal

3. Which one is a **solution**?   ❏ solitude   ❏ answer   ❏ problem

Portfolio Page

Write about an experiment that you might do involving gravity. Use at least three vocabulary words from this lesson.

SCIENCE/EXPERIMENTS

Name _____ Date _____

assess	comparison	discovery	evident	investigation
precise	procedure	simulate	solution	valid

A. Some words have more than one meaning. Choose the word that gives the best meaning for the vocabulary word as it's used in each sentence.

1. If your book is late, the library will
assess a fine. ❏ charge ❏ return ❏ examine

2. Those coupons are out of date
and no longer **valid**. ❏ sound ❏ false ❏ acceptable

3. If you dissolve salt in water, you
get a **solution**. ❏ answer ❏ question ❏ mixture

B. Each of the vocabulary words below has a suffix. Write the base word for each one. Then, use the base word in a sentence.

1. investigation _____

_____

2. discovery _____

_____

3. procedure _____

_____

C. Underline the best ending for each sentence.

1. A **comparison** is helpful in _____ .
   a. forgetting things   **b.** understanding things   **c.** renewing things

2. When something is **evident**, it is _____ .
   a. hidden   **b.** noticeable   **c.** eventful

3. If you **simulate** an event, you try to _____ .
   a. simplify it   **b.** reproduce it   **c.** eradicate it

4. You need **precise** directions to _____ .
   a. get lost   **b.** stay safe   **c.** find places

180 Essential Vocabulary Words for 5th Grade © 2009 by Linda Ward Beech, Scholastic Teaching Resources

SCIENCE/EXPERIMENTS

Name _____ Date _____

Use vocabulary words from this lesson to fill in the map. Then, add other words you know.

Words That Tell What Scientists Do

1. _____

2. _____

_____

_____

_____

Words That Name Scientific Things

3. _____

4. _____

5. _____

6. _____

7. _____

_____

Science

Words That Describe Scientific Things

8. _____   _____

9. _____   _____

10. _____   _____

STUDY SKILLS/TESTS

Name _____ Date _____

analysis	description	evaluate	maintain	mental
paraphrase	refer	reflect	skim	submit

✱ SOME WORDS ARE USEFUL TO KNOW FOR STUDYING AND TEST TAKING.

In an **analysis**, you study the parts of something to determine its nature.

A **description** is a verbal representation of something.

When you **evaluate** something, you judge it.

Maintain means "preserve."

Mental refers to the mind.

If you **paraphrase** text, you put it in your own words.

Refer means "to turn to."

When you **reflect** on something, you think about it seriously.

To **skim** is to read quickly.

If you **submit** a paper, you turn it in.

Use what you know. Write the best vocabulary word to complete each sentence.

1. Emma's _____ of her trip made us feel like we were there.

2. You can _____ a page to see if it has the information you need.

3. Be sure to put your name on the test before you _____ it.

4. Before answering an essay question, _____ on what you want to say.

5. This question asks for an _____ of the plot.

6. Although her schedule is full, Zoe tries to _____ good study habits.

7. When taking notes, Amy _____ the text.

8. You need a good _____ attitude for a test.

9. For his book report, Norman will _____ a character's actions.

10. Remember to _____ to your notes when studying for a quiz.

42

180 Essential Vocabulary Words for 5th Grade © 2009 by Linda Ward Beech, Scholastic Teaching Resources

STUDY SKILLS/TESTS

Name _____ Date _____

analysis	description	evaluate	maintain	mental
paraphrase	refer	reflect	skim	submit

A. Read each pair of words. Write a vocabulary word that has the same or almost the same meaning.

1. deliberate, contemplate   _____

2. reword, rephrase   _____

3. uphold, sustain   _____

4. offer, present   _____

5. gauge, judge   _____

6. consult, seek   _____

B. Read each question. Choose the best answer.

1. What can you **skim**?   ❐ avenue   ❐ culture   ❐ paragraph

2. Which one is **mental**?   ❐ brain   ❐ news   ❐ metal

3. Which one is an **analysis**?   ❐ question   ❐ examination   ❐ problem

4. Which one is a **description**?   ❐ betrayal   ❐ denial   ❐ portrayal

Portfolio Page

Describe how you study for a test. Use at least three vocabulary words from this lesson.

STUDY SKILLS/TESTS

Name _____ Date _____

| analysis | description | evaluate | maintain | mental |
| paraphrase | refer | reflect | skim | submit |

A. **For each word below, write a vocabulary word that is an antonym.**

1. retrieve _____

2. physical _____

3. neglect _____

B. **Some words have more than one meaning. Choose the word or phrase that gives the best meaning for the vocabulary word as it's used in each sentence.**

1. She **skimmed** across the ice. ❑ stumbled ❑ glided ❑ wandered

2. The real estate agent **evaluated** the house. ❑ appraised ❑ repaired ❑ admired

3. The test had questions of every **description**. ❑ picture ❑ word ❑ kind

4. The teacher **referred** to Robert Frost. ❑ asked ❑ reviewed ❑ mentioned

5. The mirror **reflects** her image. ❑ forms ❑ respects ❑ blots out

C. **Read the word meaning in each sentence. Then, write the vocabulary word that comes from the Greek word.**

1. The Greek word *paraphrazein* means "to show." _____

2. The Greek word *analusis* means "a releasing." _____

180 Essential Vocabulary Words for 5th Grade © 2009 by Linda Ward Beech, Scholastic Teaching Resources

Name _____ Date _____

Riddle:

What starts with T, ends with T, and is full of T?

To answer the riddle, find and shade the spaces with word pairs that are synonyms.

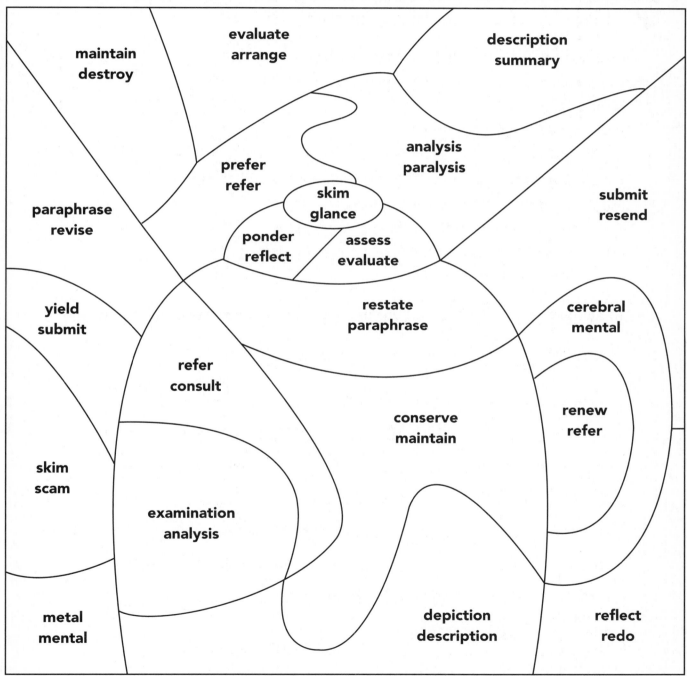

- evaluate arrange
- description summary
- maintain destroy
- analysis paralysis
- prefer refer
- skim glance
- submit resend
- paraphrase revise
- ponder reflect
- assess evaluate
- yield submit
- restate paraphrase
- cerebral mental
- refer consult
- renew refer
- conserve maintain
- skim scam
- examination analysis
- metal mental
- depiction description
- reflect redo

Answer: _____

180 Essential Vocabulary Words for 5th Grade © 2009 by Linda Ward Beech, Scholastic Teaching Resources

Name _____ Date _____

abstract	**appreciate**	**depict**	**dimension**	**illustration**
perspective	**spatial**	**technique**	**unique**	**variation**

✳ YOU USE CERTAIN WORDS WHEN YOU TALK ABOUT ART.

Abstract art has forms that are not recognizable.

If you **appreciate** a work of art, you enjoy and understand it.

Depict means "show."

A **dimension** is a measurement.

An **illustration** is a picture.

We use **perspective** to show 3-dimensional objects on flat paper.

Spatial means "having to do with space."

Technique is a method of doing something.

Unique means "one of a kind."

A **variation** is a change.

Use what you know. Write the best vocabulary word to complete each sentence.

1. Haley admired the _____ on the cover of the book she was reading.

2. At the museum, the students saw some _____ art.

3. What kind of art do you _____ when you go to a museum?

4. Kevin used several _____ of green in his painting.

5. Mrs. Elbert said that each artwork is _____ .

6. Kito used _____ to show a building in the distance in his picture.

7. Ernesto tried to _____ a rhinoceros but found it hard.

8. Working in watercolor requires a different _____ than working in oil paint.

9. The _____ of the artist's paintings were huge.

10. To work on a sculpture, Han-su had to think in _____ terms.

180 Essential Vocabulary Words for 5th Grade © 2009 by Linda Ward Beech, Scholastic Teaching Resources

Name _____ Date _____

abstract	appreciate	depict	dimension	illustration
perspective	spatial	technique	unique	variation

A. Read the first word in each row. Find and circle another word in that row that is a synonym.

1. **variation**   consistency   vibrancy   alteration   complication

2. **unique**   sole   unkind   common   uniform

3. **illustration**   text   illumination   headline   picture

4. **appreciate**   approach   apprehend   dislike   admire

5. **technique**   tendency   procedure   challenge   amateur

6. **depict**   convey   deport   deposit   compare

7. **dimension**   dilemma   discussion   division   proportion

B. Read each question. Choose the best answer.

1. Which one is not **abstract**?   ❑ mysterious   ❑ concrete   ❑ obscure

2. Which one has **perspective**?   ❑ subject   ❑ sculpture   ❑ landscape

3. Which one is **spatial**?   ❑ architecture   ❑ medicine   ❑ teaching

Portfolio Page

Write a description of one of your favorite works of art. Use at least three vocabulary words from this lesson.

Name _____ Date _____

abstract	appreciate	depict	dimension	illustration
perspective	spatial	technique	unique	variation

A. The lesson words below have suffixes. Underline the suffix in each word. Then, write a sentence using the word.

1. appreciation _____

2. abstraction _____

3. uniqueness _____

4. spatially _____

B. Write a sentence to answer each question.

1. What is something you'd like to **depict** in a painting?

_____

2. What are the **dimensions** of your classroom?

_____

3. What is your favorite book **illustration**?

_____

4. Why is **technique** important in art?

_____

C. Some words have more than one meaning. Choose the word that gives the best meaning for the vocabulary word as it's used in each sentence.

1. She performed a **variation** in the ballet. ❏ solo   ❏ change   ❏ stunt

2. Dad's **perspective** differs from mine. ❏ personality   ❏ vista   ❏ viewpoint

48

180 Essential Vocabulary Words for 5th Grade © 2009 by Linda Ward Beech, Scholastic Teaching Resources

Name _____ Date _____

Read the clues. Identify the correct vocabulary word and write it next to its clue. Then, find and circle each word in the puzzle.

C	A	B	S	T	R	A	C	T	B	K	D
V	E	D	Z	P	W	A	H	L	D	F	I
A	P	P	R	E	C	I	A	T	E	I	M
R	G	P	S	R	A	D	X	U	P	Q	E
I	L	L	U	S	T	R	A	T	I	O	N
A	M	G	N	P	W	N	R	J	C	T	S
T	B	Q	Y	E	T	I	B	C	T	Y	I
I	O	M	E	C	W	D	G	K	U	E	O
O	S	P	A	T	I	A	L	O	I	M	N
N	V	U	N	I	Q	U	E	X	O	Z	K
L	S	C	H	V	J	H	P	F	L	A	R
F	V	Z	T	E	C	H	N	I	Q	U	E

Hint:
The words can run
ACROSS
or
DOWN.

Clues

1. art with unrecognizable forms   _____

2. to admire a work of art   _____

3. a picture that accompanies text   _____

4. relating to the use of space   _____

5. singular   _____

6. a way of doing something   _____

7. a change from the usual thing   _____

8. useful in drawing scenery   _____

9. to show or describe   _____

10. the size of something   _____

Name _____ Date _____

commence	**constant**	**contemporary**	**duration**	**eventually**
interval	**mature**	**periodic**	**previous**	**temporary**

✱ YOU USE CERTAIN WORDS WHEN YOU REFER TO TIME.

Commence means begin.

If something is **constant**, it remains the same.

Contemporary means "current."

The period of time in which something happens is the **duration**.

Eventually means "happening at some future time."

An **interval** is a period of time between two events.

Something that is **mature** has reached its full growth.

Periodic means "happening at regular intervals."

Previous means "at an earlier time."

If something is **temporary**, it is for a limited time.

Use what you know. Write the best vocabulary word to complete each sentence.

1. It will be 30 years before that tree is _____ .

2. Walter got a drink of water in the _____ between speakers.

3. The _____ of Fay's visit was short.

4. The performance will _____ soon.

5. Malik got a _____ job before he started college.

6. Carol updated her wardrobe so it was more _____ .

7. Cindy scored much higher on this test than she did on the

_____ one.

8. Felice and Lea are good friends and _____ companions.

9. We hope their puppy will calm down _____ .

10. During the storm, there were _____ bursts of thunder.

50

180 Essential Vocabulary Words for 5th Grade © 2009 by Linda Ward Beech, Scholastic Teaching Resources

Name _____ Date _____

commence	constant	contemporary	duration	eventually
interval	mature	periodic	previous	temporary

A. Read the vocabulary word. Underline the word that is a synonym. Circle the word that is an antonym.

1. **contemporary**   old-fashioned   modern   comfortable   casual

2. **previous**   preview   prior   devious   following

3. **commence**   commend   end   start   forget

4. **mature**   young   motherly   grown   natural

5. **temporary**   tempered   orderly   limited   permanent

6. **constant**   continuous   connected   agreeable   inconstant

B. Read each question. Choose the best answer.

1. Which one is an **interval**?   ❑ break   ❑ interview   ❑ return

2. Which one is **periodic**?   ❑ perimeter   ❑ full moon   ❑ first aid

3. Which one is a **duration**?   ❑ team   ❑ turn   ❑ term

4. Which one is **eventually**?   ❑ equally   ❑ timely   ❑ ultimately

Portfolio Page

Write a description of a storm. Use at least three vocabulary words from the lesson.

Name _____ Date _____

| commence | constant | contemporary | duration | eventually |
| interval | mature | periodic | previous | temporary |

A. Some words have more than one meaning. Choose the word or phrase that gives the best meaning for the vocabulary word as it's used in each sentence. Use a dictionary if needed.

1. She is my **contemporary**. ❑ current friend ❑ same age ❑ older relative

2. This loan has **matured**. ❑ is due ❑ gotten ripe ❑ grown old

3. There were **periodic** shouts of laughter from the crowd. ❑ cyclical ❑ constant ❑ occasional

B. The lesson words below have suffixes. Underline the suffix in each word. Then, write a sentence using the word.

1. temporarily

_____

2. commencement

_____

3. previously

_____

C. Underline the best ending for each sentence.

1. Knowing the **duration** of an appointment can help you _____ .

    a. waste your time   **b.** plan your time   **c.** call time out

2. By studying hard, students can **eventually** _____ .

    a. forget their grades   **b.** lower their grades   **c.** improve their grades

3. You might use an **interval** at a dance to _____ .

    a. change clothes   **b.** get refreshments   **c.** begin dancing

4. A **constant** noise during a test is likely to become _____ .

    a. distracting   **b.** amusing   **c.** welcome

180 Essential Vocabulary Words for 5th Grade © 2009 by Linda Ward Beech, Scholastic Teaching Resources

Name _____ Date _____

Read each clue. Write the correct vocabulary word in each set of boxes. Then, write the letters from the shaded boxes in order on the lines below to find the mystery word.

1. intermittent ☐ ☐ ▨ ☐ ☐ ☐ ☐ ☐

2. describes an intermission ☐ ☐ ☐ ▨ ☐ ☐ ☐ ☐

3. unchanging ▨ ☐ ☐ ☐ ☐ ☐ ☐ ☐

4. a length of time ☐ ☐ ▨ ☐ ☐ ☐ ☐ ☐

5. not permanent ☐ ▨ ☐ ☐ ☐ ☐ ☐ ☐

6. fully grown ☐ ▨ ☐ ☐ ☐

7. in a future time ☐ ☐ ☐ ☐ ▨ ☐ ☐ ☐ ☐ ☐

8. in an earlier time ☐ ☐ ☐ ☐ ▨ ☐ ☐ ☐

9. initiate or inaugurate ☐ ▨ ☐ ☐ ☐ ☐ ☐ ☐

10. something happening now ☐ ☐ ▨ ☐ ☐ ☐ ☐ ☐ ☐ ☐ ☐ ☐

Mystery Word

Some of the best time is spent in ___ ___ ___ ___ ___ ___ ___ ___ ___ ___ .

Name _____ Date _____

external	flexible	injure	internal	normal
persist	prohibit	random	react	stable

✱ YOU USE CERTAIN WORDS WHEN YOU TALK ABOUT HEALTH AND SAFETY.

Something that is **external** is outside.

Flexible means "easily bent."

If you **injure** yourself, you cause harm.

Something that is **internal** is inside.

Normal means "usual."

If symptoms **persist**, they last.

Prohibit means "forbid."

Something that is **random** has no pattern or purpose.

When you act in response to something, you **react**.

Stable means "steady, safe, or likely to continue."

Use what you know. Write the best vocabulary word to complete each sentence.

1. The patient's temperature was _____ .

2. Because it is dangerous, the rules _____ us from swimming alone.

3. If her cold symptoms _____ , Lily will call the doctor.

4. Without an X-ray, the doctor could only see Judy's _____ injuries.

5. The gym teacher demonstrated exercises to make us more _____ .

6. Germs spread in a _____ way when Myra sneezed.

7. Be careful or you'll _____ yourself with that sharp tool.

8. Arlo's condition has improved, and he is _____ .

9. Your stomach is an _____ organ.

10. When the ball comes at her, Ming must _____ quickly.

180 Essential Vocabulary Words for 5th Grade © 2009 by Linda Ward Beech, Scholastic Teaching Resources

HEALTH/SAFETY

Name _____ Date _____

external	flexible	injure	internal	normal
persist	prohibit	random	react	stable

A. Read the first word in each row. Circle the other words in the row that have similar meanings.

1. **random**   orderly   chance   haphazard

2. **internal**   inner   interior   upper

3. **stable**   enduring   uncertain   permanent

4. **persist**   persevere   insist   perplex

5. **external**   excellent   outer   exterior

6. **flexible**   fleeting   supple   pliable

7. **injure**   damage   infer   hurt

B. Read each question. Choose the best answer.

1. Which body temperature is **normal**?   ❏ 96.8°F   ❏ 100°F   ❏ 98.6°F

2. What is **prohibited** in most places?   ❏ smelling   ❏ smoking   ❏ smiling

3. How do children **react** to something that hurts?   ❏ laugh   ❏ clap   ❏ cry

Portfolio Page

Write a list of health and safety rules that would be useful in your school. Use at least three vocabulary words from this lesson.

Name _____ Date _____

| external | flexible | injure | internal | normal |
| persist | prohibit | random | react | stable |

A. Add one of these prefixes to each vocabulary word below. Then, use the new word in a sentence.

ab-   un-   in-

1. flexible   _____

_____

2. normal   _____

_____

3. stable   _____

_____

B. The lesson words below have suffixes. Underline the suffix in each word. Then, write a sentence using the word.

1. reaction

_____

2. persistence

_____

3. injury

_____

4. internalize

_____

C. Write a vocabulary word that is an antonym for each word below.

1.   planned   2.   internal   3.   allow

_____   _____   _____

180 Essential Vocabulary Words for 5th Grade © 2009 by Linda Ward Beech, Scholastic Teaching Resources

Name _____ Date _____

Play the So Is Game.

Complete each sentence with a vocabulary word from the lesson.

1. *Bendable* means _____ and so does *pliant*.

2. A cyclist must be _____ on his equipment and so must a skier.

3. Skin is _____ and so are fingernails.

4. Sniffles may _____ and so may a cough.

5. A sign can _____ and so can a gate.

6. A hammer can _____ you and so can a saw.

7. Your heart is _____ and so is your liver.

8. *Customary* means _____ and so does *habitual*.

9. An accident is _____ and so is luck.

10. People _____ to loud noises and so do animals.

Name _____ Date _____

bias	**demonstration**	**indifference**	**individual**	**input**
participation	**reform**	**resolution**	**tolerance**	**voluntary**

✴ SOME WORDS ARE USED OFTEN WHEN TALKING ABOUT CITIZENSHIP.

A **bias** is a prejudice.

A **demonstration** is a public display.

Indifference is a lack of concern.

An **individual** is a distinct person.

Input is information that you add to something.

Participation is taking part in something.

When you **reform** something, you correct it.

A **resolution** is a decision.

Tolerance is recognizing and respecting others.

Voluntary means "done of your own free will."

Use what you know. Write a vocabulary word to complete each sentence.

1. When people don't bother to vote in an election, they show _____ .

2. Some people held a _____ for better wages.

3. During the meeting Estela showed _____ for everyone's point of view.

4. An important part of democracy is the _____ of its citizens.

5. Each _____ has certain rights.

6. The committee passed a _____ about the issue.

7. Meg helps out in the library on a _____ basis.

8. Simon added his _____ to the discussion.

9. Dr. Stone is worried about our local government and thinks we need some

_____ .

10. Milt's neighbor has a _____ against cats because he's allergic.

180 Essential Vocabulary Words for 5th Grade © 2009 by Linda Ward Beech, Scholastic Teaching Resources

Name _____ Date _____

bias	demonstration	indifference	individual	input
participation	reform	resolution	tolerance	voluntary

A. Read each pair of words. Write a vocabulary word that means the same or almost the same thing.

1. person, someone _____

2. prejudice, influence _____

3. rally, march _____

4. improve, rectify _____

5. insensibility, apathy _____

6. acceptance, openmindedness _____

7. cooperation, collaboration _____

B. Read each question. Choose the best answer.

1. Which one is **input**? ❒ damage ❒ data ❒ dawn

2. Which one is a **resolution**? ❒ plan ❒ plane ❒ plain

3. Which one is **voluntary**? ❒ illness ❒ mishap ❒ gift

Portfolio Page

Write an editorial for a school newspaper about good citizenship in the classroom. Use at least three vocabulary words from this lesson.

CITIZENSHIP

Name _____ Date _____

bias	demonstration	indifference	individual	input
participation	reform	resolution	tolerance	voluntary

A. For each number, read the words. Shade the word in one of the bottom boxes that is an antonym of the word in the top box.

1.
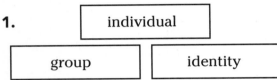

individual

group   identity

2.
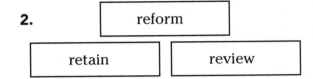

reform

retain   review

3.
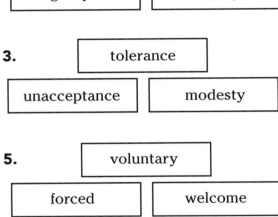

tolerance

unacceptance   modesty

4.
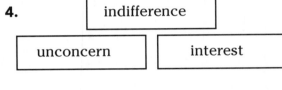

indifference

unconcern   interest

5.

voluntary

forced   welcome

6.
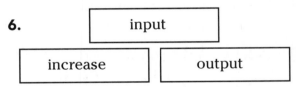

input

increase   output

B. The vocabulary words below contain a suffix. Write the base word for each one. Then, use the base word in a sentence.

1. resolution   _____

_____

2. participation   _____

_____

3. demonstration   _____

_____

C. Write a sentence to answer the question.

1. Why might you try to change a **bias** that someone has? _____

_____

180 Essential Vocabulary Words for 5th Grade © 2009 by Linda Ward Beech, Scholastic Teaching Resources

Name _____ Date _____

An analogy is a comparison based on how things are related to one another. Decide how the first set of words is related. Then, use the best vocabulary word from this lesson to complete each of these analogies.

Example: Logical is to reasonable as continuing is to ongoing.

1. Required is to optional as

mandatory is to ___ ___ ___ ___ ___ ___ ___ ___ ___ .

2. Impartial is to partial as

neutral is to ___ ___ ___ ___ ___ ___ .

3. Thought is to idea as

suggestion is to ___ ___ ___ ___ ___ .

4. Team is to group as

player is to ___ ___ ___ ___ ___ ___ ___ ___ ___ ___ .

5. Preserve is to change as

maintain is to ___ ___ ___ ___ ___ ___ .

6. Decide is to decision as

resolve is to ___ ___ ___ ___ ___ ___ ___ ___ ___ .

7. Interest is to concern as

disinterest is to ___ ___ ___ ___ ___ ___ ___ ___ ___ ___ .

8. Respect is to civility as

acceptance is to ___ ___ ___ ___ ___ ___ ___ ___ ___ .

9. Disapproval is to protest as

objection is to ___ ___ ___ ___ ___ ___ ___ ___ ___ ___ ___ .

10. Giving is to contributing as

involvement is ___ ___ ___ ___ ___ ___ ___ ___ ___ ___ ___ .

DISCUSSION

Name _____ Date _____

alter	assure	confer	confirm	engage
explanation	indicate	obvious	positive	probe

✱ SOME WORDS DESCRIBE WHAT HAPPENS IN A DISCUSSION.

If you **alter** something, you change it.

Assure means "make free of doubt."

When you **confer** with others, you talk to them to get information and advice.

Confirm means "make certain."

If you **engage** someone's attention, you hold it.

An **explanation** is a clarification.

To **indicate** is to point out.

Something that is easily understood is **obvious**.

Something that is **positive** is favorable.

If you **probe**, you examine.

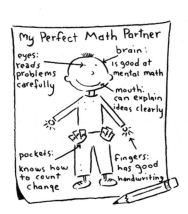

Use what you know. Write the best vocabulary word to complete each sentence.

1. Alonso gave the class an _____ of the plans for the school fair.

2. He was pleased because Nan's response was very _____ .

3. However, Jerry wanted to _____ the location of the food booth.

4. He _____ the class by outlining his reasons.

5. He _____ the place where the booth could go.

6. Laura wanted to _____ a little more into the idea.

7. Sara _____ Jerry that the committee would consider his idea.

8. She and the others _____ about the suggestion.

9. It was _____ to them that Jerry had a good point.

10. Finally, they _____ that the change would be made.

180 Essential Vocabulary Words for 5th Grade © 2009 by Linda Ward Beech, Scholastic Teaching Resources

DISCUSSION

Name _____ Date _____

alter	assure	confer	confirm	engage
explanation	indicate	obvious	positive	probe

A. Read each pair words. Write a vocabulary word that means the same or almost the same thing.

1. evident, clear _____

2. attract, hold _____

3. ensure, guarantee _____

4. affirmative, good _____

5. examine, question _____

6. consult, discuss _____

B. Read each question. Choose the best answer.

1. What might you **confirm**?   ❒ applause   ❒ appointment   ❒ apple

2. Which one **indicates**?   ❒ sparrow   ❒ root   ❒ arrow

3. Which is an **explanation**?   ❒ amount   ❒ account   ❒ fountain

4. What might you **alter**?   ❒ belief   ❒ beneath   ❒ relief

Portfolio Page

Write a dialogue for a discussion about a class event. Use at least three vocabulary words from this lesson.

DISCUSSION

Name _____ Date _____

alter	assure	confer	confirm	engage
explanation	indicate	obvious	positive	probe

A. Add one of these prefixes to each vocabulary word below.
Then, use the new word in a sentence.

re-   dis-

1. **engage** _____

_____

2. **assure** _____

_____

3. **confirm** _____

_____

B. Underline the best ending for each sentence.

1. To **indicate** their current location, the guide _____ .

   a. pointed to the map   **b.** drove to the national park   **c.** asked for directions

2. Justina provided an **explanation** because her classmates were _____ .

   a. excited   **b.** confused   **c.** bored

3. The workers needed to **confer** with the manager to _____ .

   a. choose a favorite sports team   **b.** have lunch   **c.** find out details about the project

4. Because two extra guests showed up for the party, he had to **alter** _____ .

   a. the curtains   **b.** the table setting   **c.** the invitation

C. Write a vocabulary word that is an antonym for each word below.

1.   negative   2.   hidden   3.   ignore

_____   _____   _____

180 Essential Vocabulary Words for 5th Grade © 2009 by Linda Ward Beech, Scholastic Teaching Resources

Name _____ Date _____

Read the clues. Then, complete the puzzle using vocabulary words from this lesson.

Across

1. engross

5. adjust or change

8. point out

9. favorable

10. investigate

Down

2. convince

3. something that answers questions

4. discuss

6. verify

7. apparent

Name _____ Date _____

collapse	contact	dedicate	emerge	equip
inherit	insert	occupy	resist	unify

✱ A VERB IS A WORD THAT SHOWS ACTION IN A SENTENCE. THESE ACTION VERBS ARE USEFUL TO KNOW IN SCHOOL.

If things **collapse**, they cave in.

To **contact** is to get in touch with.

If you **dedicate** yourself to something, you commit to it.

Emerge means "come into view."

When you supply what is needed for something, you **equip** for that purpose.

To **inherit** is to receive something from someone else.

If you **insert** a sentence into a paragraph, you put it in.

If you **occupy** something, you are in it.

When you **resist**, you don't give in.

Unify means "unite."

Use what you know. Write the best vocabulary word to complete each sentence.

1. Paula will _____ everyone by phone.

2. Rod hopes to _____ his brother's bike when he is older.

3. The clerk helped _____ us for the campout.

4. Blaine _____ the tempting sweets.

5. The sand castle _____ when the waves hit it.

6. Two people cannot _____ the same chair.

7. Hans plans to _____ himself to swimming this summer.

8. After the argument, the coach tried to _____ the members of the team.

9. When the cuckoo clock strikes the hour, a bird will _____ .

10. To open the door, _____ the key in the lock and turn it.

180 Essential Vocabulary Words for 5th Grade © 2009 by Linda Ward Beech, Scholastic Teaching Resources

Name _____ Date _____

collapse	contact	dedicate	emerge	equip
inherit	insert	occupy	resist	unify

A. Draw a line from each vocabulary word to match it with a synonym.

1. **dedicate**   **a.** fall

2. **emerge**   **b.** provide

3. **equip**   **c.** withstand

4. **resist**   **d.** add

5. **occupy**   **e.** devote

6. **collapse**   **f.** inhabit

7. **insert**   **g.** appear

8. **unify**   **h.** consolidate

B. Read each question. Choose the best answer.

1. Which one would you **contact**?   ❏ stranger   ❏ foe   ❏ friend

2. Which one do people usually **inherit**?   ❏ sleep   ❏ money   ❏ habitat

Portfolio Page

Write a paragraph about an extracurricular activity that you enjoy at school. Use at least three vocabulary words from this lesson.

Name _____ Date _____

collapse	contact	dedicate	emerge	equip
inherit	insert	occupy	resist	unify

A. Many words can be used as more than one part of speech. Circle *noun* or *verb* for each word.

1. The **collapse** of the tent created problems for us.   noun   verb

2. Kali will **collapse** her umbrella when the rain stops.   noun   verb

3. Mrs. Ross still has to **contact** us about the school trip.   noun   verb

4. He is our **contact** in case of emergency.   noun   verb

B. Some words have more than one meaning. Choose the word or phrase that gives the best meaning for the vocabulary word as it's used in each sentence.

1. The team **resisted** the attack.   ❏ invited   ❏ opposed   ❏ permitted

2. She **dedicated** the book to her daughter.
    ❏ gave   ❏ opened   ❏ addressed

3. Alice **emerged** as a strong batter.
    ❏ entered   ❏ withdrew   ❏ attracted notice

4. What do you do to **occupy** your time?
    ❏ fill   ❏ inhabit   ❏ take over

C. Write a sentence to answer each question.

1. Why might you **insert** words into a report?

_____

2. How would you **equip** your family for a hike?

_____

3. What would be a reason to try to **unify** two groups?

_____

4. What is a characteristic that you have **inherited**?

_____

180 Essential Vocabulary Words for 5th Grade © 2009 by Linda Ward Beech, Scholastic Teaching Resources

Name _____ Date _____

Read the clues. Complete the puzzle using the vocabulary words from this lesson.

1. say "no"

2. take up space

3. appear

4. furnish

5. commit

6. fall apart

7. receive someone's possessions

8. bring together

9. get in touch with

10. add something in

1. ___ ___ **S** ___ ___ ___

2. **O** ___ ___ ___ ___

3. ___ **M** ___ ___ ___ ___

4. **E** ___ ___ ___ ___

5. ___ ___ ___ ___ ___ **A** ___ ___

6. **C** ___ ___ ___ ___ ___ ___ ___

7. ___ ___ ___ ___ ___ **T**

8. ___ ___ **I** ___ ___

9. **O** ___ ___ ___ ___ ___

10. ___ **N** ___ ___ ___ ___

ADJECTIVES

Name _____ Date _____

authentic	definite	dramatic	fundamental	general
identical	indirect	legendary	remarkable	secure

✳ AN ADJECTIVE IS A WORD THAT MODIFIES A NOUN OR PRONOUN.

If something is **authentic**, it is the real thing.

Something that is **definite** is clearly defined.

Dramatic refers to something with drama.

Fundamental means "basic."

Something that is **general** is true in most cases.

Identical things are exactly alike.

When something is **indirect**, it is not straightforward.

Someone or something **legendary** is famous.

Something that is **remarkable** is worthy of notice.

Secure means "free from danger."

Use what you know. Write the best vocabulary word to complete each sentence.

1. Have you noticed that the socks in a pair are _____ ?

2. The light hits the painting at an _____ angle.

3. Ms. Lanza gave us a _____ time to arrive for the surprise party.

4. Mr. Cruz's delicious, homemade jams are _____.

5. When Brian saw the old coin, he wondered if it was _____ .

6. The bus driver made sure that the students were _____
in their seatbelts.

7. Alice made a _____ entrance on the stage.

8. We began by learning some _____ things about rock climbing.

9. The story she wrote is quite _____ for her age.

10. In _____, the class didn't have homework over the weekend.

180 Essential Vocabulary Words for 5th Grade © 2009 by Linda Ward Beech, Scholastic Teaching Resources

Name _____ Date _____

authentic	definite	dramatic	fundamental	general
identical	indirect	legendary	remarkable	secure

A. Read the first word in each row. Underline the word in that row that is a synonym. Circle the word that is an antonym.

1. **dramatic**   bland   dangerous   theatrical

2. **secure**   safe   loose   threatened

3. **definite**   curious   vague   precise

4. **identical**   regular   same   dissimilar

5. **indirect**   slanted   straight   unreasonable

6. **fundamental**   unnecessary   elementary   wealthy

7. **remarkable**   extraordinary renewable   uninteresting

B. Read each sentence. Choose the best answer.

1. Which one is **legendary**?   ❏ usher   ❏ stagehand   ❏ star

2. Which one is **general**?   ❏ typical   ❏ unusual   ❏ magical

3. Which one is **authentic**?   ❏ copy   ❏ original   ❏ imitation

Portfolio Page

Write an ad for a new school product. Use at least three vocabulary words from this lesson.

ADJECTIVES

Name _____ Date _____

authentic	definite	dramatic	fundamental	general
identical	indirect	legendary	remarkable	secure

A. Add one of these suffixes to the vocabulary words below. Then, use each new word in a sentence.   -ity   -ion

1. secure   _____

_____

2. authentic   _____

_____

3. definite   _____

_____

B. Underline the best ending for each sentence.

1. Someone who makes a **dramatic** entrance wants _____ .

   a. inattention   **b.** suggestions   **c.** recognition

2. **General** admission to a show is usually for _____ .

   a. everyone   **b.** children   **c.** seniors

3. When two people are **identical**, they are _____ .

   a. cousins   **b.** twins   **c.** friends

4. If you travel by an **indirect** route, the trip will be _____ .

   a. shorter   **b.** faster   **c.** longer

5. If you don't learn the **fundamental** rules of a game, you will _____ .

   a. win the game   **b.** make mistakes   **c.** score points

6. When you do something **remarkable**, it often brings _____ .

   a. approval   **b.** dissent   **c.** relaxation

7. When someone is **legendary**, that person is usually _____ .

   a. forgotten   **b.** average   **c.** outstanding

180 Essential Vocabulary Words for 5th Grade © 2009 by Linda Ward Beech, Scholastic Teaching Resources

ADJECTIVES

Name _____ Date _____

Play the Word Clue Game.

Write the best vocabulary word for each clue. Use each word only once.

Clues	Vocabulary Words
1. is a synonym for *genuine*	
2. is the opposite of *specific*	
3. has the word *mental* in it	
4. from the Latin word *identicus* meaning "identity"	
5. can mean "exact"	
6. begins with a prefix that means "not"	
7. is related to *drama* and *dramatize*	
8. is an antonym for *endangered*	
9. can mean "uncommon"	
10. means "famous"	

Name _____ Date _____

authority	development	ideal	influence	output
phase	proposal	scope	structure	target

✳ A NOUN IS A WORD THAT NAMES A PERSON, PLACE, OR THING. THESE NOUNS ARE USEFUL TO KNOW IN SCHOOL.

Authority is the power to do something.

A **development** is something that has happened or unfolded.

An **ideal** is a model of perfection.

Influence is the ability to make things happen.

Output is something that is produced.

A **phase** is a stage in a process.

A **proposal** is an offer.

The **scope** of something is its range.

A **structure** is something that has been built.

A **target** is something you aim for.

Use what you know. Write the best vocabulary word to complete each sentence.

1. Dad made a _____ for a family outing.

2. The customer used his _____ to get good seats at the restaurant.

3. They are in the first _____ of building a house.

4. Sonia has high _____ and tries to live up to them.

5. The ranger has the _____ to make sure rules are followed in the park.

6. The _____ of this project is enormous.

7. Damon's _____ is the result of hard work.

8. That bridge is an imposing _____ .

9. Mr. Clancy had a _____ of getting 20 new customers a week at his store.

10. Harriet was surprised to read the new _____ in the mystery.

180 Essential Vocabulary Words for 5th Grade © 2009 by Linda Ward Beech, Scholastic Teaching Resources

Name _____ Date _____

authority	development	ideal	influence	output
phase	proposal	scope	structure	target

A. Read the first word in each row. Circle the other words in that row with similar meanings.

1. **proposal**   suggestion   plan   proof

2. **phase**   phrase   stage   step

3. **scope**   breadth   extent   scuba

4. **influence**   instruction   impression   effect

5. **target**   arrow   goal   intention

6. **authority**   power   jurisdiction   author

7. **ideal**   idleness   standard   model

8. **development**   device   evolution   outcome

B. Read each question. Choose the best answer.

1. Which one is an **output**?   ❏ outsider   ❏ product   ❏ ingredient

2. Which one is a **structure**?   ❏ tower   ❏ garden   ❏ beach

Portfolio Page

Write a news article about a new building in your community. Use at least three vocabulary words from this lesson.

180 Essential Vocabulary Words for 5th Grade © 2009 by Linda Ward Beech, Scholastic Teaching Resources

NOUNS

Name _____ Date _____

authority	development	ideal	influence	output
phase	proposal	scope	structure	target

A. Some words have more than one meaning. Choose the word that gives the best meaning for the vocabulary word as it's used in each sentence.

1. The computer produced some interesting **output**.

   ❐ information   ❐ problems   ❐ energy

2. The scientist studied the microbe through a **scope**.

   ❐ telescope   ❐ periscope   ❐ microscope

B. Many words can be used as more than one part of speech. Circle *noun*, *verb*, or *adjective* for each vocabulary word.

1. Jessica tried to **influence** her dad's decision.	noun	verb	adjective
2. The mayor's **influence** helped get the law passed.	noun	verb	adjective
3. We will **target** Monday for our departure.	noun	verb	adjective
4. What is our **target** for the fundraising?	noun	verb	adjective
5. The company is going to **phase** out this model.	noun	verb	adjective
6. Kent took notes during the first **phase** of the lecture.	noun	verb	adjective
7. They discussed how to **structure** the deal.	noun	verb	adjective
8. Our school is a large **structure**.	noun	verb	adjective
9. Always being honest is an **ideal** Brenda holds.	noun	verb	adjective
10. He is the **ideal** brother.	noun	verb	adjective

C. Each of the lesson words below has a suffix. Write the base word for each.

1.   development   2.   authority   3.   proposal

_____   _____   _____

180 Essential Vocabulary Words for 5th Grade © 2009 by Linda Ward Beech, Scholastic Teaching Resources

Name _____ Date _____

Complete a chain for each word. In each circle, write a word that is related to the word just before it. An example is done for you.

1. (target) (aim) (work) (struggle) (success)

2. (ideal) ( ) ( ) ( ) ( )

3. (scope) ( ) ( ) ( ) ( )

4. (authority) ( ) ( ) ( ) ( )

5. (influence) ( ) ( ) ( ) ( )

6. (output) ( ) ( ) ( ) ( )

7. (phase) ( ) ( ) ( ) ( )

8. (proposal) ( ) ( ) ( ) ( )

9. (structure) ( ) ( ) ( ) ( )

10. (development) ( ) ( ) ( ) ( )

180 Essential Vocabulary Words for 5th Grade © 2009 by Linda Ward Beech, Scholastic Teaching Resources

LESSON 1

Page 6: 1. intermediate 2. essential 3. enroll 4. translation 5. sections 6. discipline 7. information 8. integrate 9. supervise 10. promote **Page 7: A.** 1.enlist, register 2. fundamental, indispensable 3. part, portion 4. control, oversee 5. unify, consolidate 6. data, knowledge 7. progress, advance **B.** 1. middle 2. express 3. training **Page 8: A.** 1.–5. Sentences will vary. 1. supervision 2. translator 3. intermediary 4. enrollment 5. integration **B.** 1.–5. Sentences will vary. **Page 9:** 1. essential 2. intermediate 3. section 4. discipline 5. promote 6. information 7. translation 8. integrate 9. supervise 10. enroll

LESSON 2

Page 10: 1. classics 2. figurative 3. motive 4. insight 5. analogy 6. introduction 7. narrative 8. diction 9. infer 10. foreshadowed **Page 11: A.** 1. diction 2. foreshadow 3. infer 4. insight 5. introduction 6. motive **B.** 1. past 2. fanciful 3. similarity 4. storybook **Page 12: A.** 1. analogy 2. diction 3. infer 4. insight **B.** 1. figurative 2. introduction **C.** 1.–4. Sentences will vary. **Page 13:** 1. narrative 2. motive 3. classic 4. diction 5. infer 6. analogy 7. introduction 8. foreshadow 9. figurative 10. insight

LESSON 3

Page 14: 1. convince 2. inspiration 3. abbreviation 4. compound 5. composition 6. header 7. modifies 8. revision 9. clarify 10. specific **Page 15: A.** 1. e 2. d 3. g 4. b 5. f 6. c 7. a **B.** 1. top 2. classroom 3. meaning **Page 16: A.** 1. dissuade 2. footer 3. confuse 4. vague 5. simple 6. preserve **B.** 1.–4. Sentences will vary. 1. inspire 2. abbreviate 3. revise 4. compose **Page 17:** 1. clarify 2. revision 3. composition 4. modify 5. compound 6. convince 7. abbreviation 8. specific 9. header 10. inspiration; Mystery Word: communicate.

LESSON 4

Page 18: 1. expository 2. statement 3. rephrases 4. examine 5. glossary 6. contrast 7. excerpts 8. acronym 9. cited 10. acquired **Page 19: A.** 1. get, obtain 2. study, observe 3. restate, reword 4. vary, differ 5. informative, revelatory **B.** 1. declarative 2. modem 3. passage 4. dictionary 5. accuracy **Page 20: A.** 1. record 2. honored 3. questioned **B.** 1. noun 2. verb 3. verb 4. noun **C.** 1.–5. Sentences will vary. **Page 21:** 1. expository 2. glossary 3. examine 4. statement 5. acronym 6. excerpt 7. cite 8. acquire 9. rephrase 10. contrast

LESSON 5

Page 22: 1. fund 2. scarce 3. asset 4. credit 5. computed 6. inventory 7. invest 8. income 9. minimum 10. finance **Page 23: A.** 1. scarce 2. compute 3. asset 4. minimum 5. income 6. inventory **B.** 1. to gain 2. charge 3. savings 4. money **Page 24: A.** 1. maximum, minimum 2. debit, credit 3. plentiful, scarce 4. expenses, income 5. invest, divest 6. liability, asset **B.** 1. supply 2. pay for **C.** 1. c 2. b **Page 25: Across:** 2. fund 6. inventory 7. income 8. finance

10. compute **Down:** 1. invest 3. minimum 4. credit 5. scarce 9. asset

LESSON 6

Page 26: 1. innocent 2. military 3. elevation 4. transferred 5. established 6. employ 7. survey 8. issues 9. property 10. profession **Page 27: A.** 1. elevation 2. profession 3. establish **B.** 1. synonym—hire; antonym—fire 2. synonym—blameless; antonym—guilty 3. synonym—move; antonym—remain **C.** 1. yours 2. questionnaire 3. armament 4. taxes **Page 28: A.** 1. confirmed 2. use 3. looked over 4. characteristic 5. advancement 6. make available **B.** 1.–2. Sentences will vary. **C.** 1. noun 2. adjective 3. adjective 4. noun **Page 29:** 1. military 2. elevation 3. transfer 4. issue 5. profession 6. employ 7. establish 8. survey 9. innocent 10. property

LESSON 7

Page 30: 1. democracy 2. guarantees 3. executive 4. judicial 5. legislative 6. amendment 7. consent 8. policies 9. minority 10. diverse **Page 31: A.** 1. president 2. few 3. representative 4. lawmaker 5. judge **B.** 1. assent, concur 2. different, dissimilar 3. revision, improvement 4. program, strategy 5. pledge, assurance **Page 32: A.** 1. minority 2. diverse 3. consent 4. guarantee **B.** (Possible answers are provided for Another Related Word) 1. policy, politics 2. judicial, judiciary 3. executive, executor 4. amendment, amend 5. democracy, democrat 6. legislative, legislator **Page 33:** 1. policy 2. legislative 3. consent 4. democracy 5. executive 6. guarantee 7. minority 8. judicial 9. diverse 10. amendment(s)

LESSON 8

Page 34: 1. erosion 2. body 3. elements 4. distinct 5. medical 6. convert 7. technical 8. function 9. formula 10. evolved **Page 35: A.** 1. d 2. c 3. a 4. f 5. b 6. e **B.** 1. gold 2. wind 3. digital 4. bobcat **Page 36: A.** 1. event 2. unfolded 3. mixture 4. environment 5. collection **B.** 1. distinct 2. erosion **C.** 1. convert 2. technical 3. medical **Page 37:** 1. technical 2. formula 3. body 4. distinct 5. medical 6. erosion 7. evolve 8. convert 9. function 10. element

LESSON 9

Page 38: 1. comparison 2. valid 3. evident 4. precise 5. assessed 6. procedure 7. simulate 8. investigation 9. discovery 10. solution **Page 39: A.** 1. assess 2. investigation 3. simulate **B.** 1. synonym—accurate; antonym—vague 2. synonym—plain; antonym—unclear 3. synonym—true; antonym—ineffective 4. synonym—finding; antonym—loss **C.** 1. differences 2. plan 3. answer **Page 40: A.** 1. charge 2. acceptable 3. mixture **B.** 1.–3. Sentences will vary. 1. investigate 2. discover 3. proceed **C.** 1. b 2. b 3. b 4. c **Page 41:** 1. assess 2. simulate 3. comparison 4. discovery 5. investigation 6. procedure 7. solution 8. evident 9. precise 10. valid

LESSON 10

Page 42: 1. description 2. skim 3. submit 4. reflect 5. analysis 6. maintain 7. paraphrases 8. mental

9. evaluate 10. refer **Page 43: A.** 1. reflect 2. paraphrase
3. maintain 4. submit 5. evaluate 6. refer **B.** 1. paragraph
2. brain 3. examination 4. portrayal **Page 44: A.** 1. submit
2. mental 3. maintain **B.** 1. glided 2. appraised 3. kind
4. mentioned 5. forms **C.** 1. paraphrase 2. analysis
Page 45: Riddle answer: teapot. Synonym pairs: skim,
glance; ponder, reflect; assess, evaluate; yield, submit;
refer, consult; restate, paraphrase; conserve, maintain;
cerebral, mental; examination, analysis; depiction,
description

LESSON 11

Page 46: 1. illustration 2. abstract 3. appreciate
4. variations 5. unique 6. perspective 7. depict
8. technique 9. dimensions 10. spatial **Page 47:**
A. 1. alteration 2. sole 3. picture 4. admire 5. procedure
6. convey 7. proportion **B.** 1. concrete 2. landscape
3. architecture **Page 48: A.** 1.–4. Sentences will vary.
1. appreciation 2. abstraction 3. uniqueness 4. spatially
B. 1.–4. Sentences will vary. **C.** 1. solo 2. viewpoint
Page 49: 1. abstract 2. appreciate 3. illustration 4. spatial
5. unique 6. technique 7. variation 8. perspective 9. depict
10. dimension

LESSON 12

Page 50: 1. mature 2. interval 3. duration 4. commence
5. temporary 6. contemporary 7. previous 8. constant
9. eventually 10. periodic **Page 51: A.** 1. synonym—
modern; antonym—old-fashioned 2. synonym—prior;
antonym—following 3. synonym—start; antonym—end
4. synonym—grown; antonym—young 5. synonym—
limited; antonym—permanent 6. synonym—continuous;
antonym—inconstant **B.** 1. break 2. full moon 3. term
4. ultimately **Page 52: A.** 1. same age 2. is due
3. occasional **B.** 1.–3. Sentences will vary. 1. temporarily
2. commencement 3. previously **C.** 1. b 2. c 3. b 4. a
Page 53: 1. periodic 2. interval 3. constant 4. duration
5. temporary 6. mature 7. eventually 8. previous
9. commence 10. contemporary; Mystery Word: recreation

LESSON 13

Page 54: 1. normal 2. prohibit 3. persist 4. external
5. flexible 6. random 7. injure 8. stable 9. internal 10. react
Page 55: A. 1. chance, haphazard 2. inner, interior
3. enduring, permanent 4. persevere, insist 5. outer,
exterior 6. supple, pliable 7. damage, hurt **B.** 1. 98.6°F
2. smoking 3. cry **Page 56: A.** 1.–3. Sentences will vary.
1. inflexible 2. abnormal 3. unstable **B.** 1.–4. Sentences will
vary. 1. reaction 2. persistence 3. injury 4. internalize
C. 1. random 2. external 3. prohibit **Page 57:** 1. flexible
2. stable 3. external 4. persist 5. prohibit 6. injure
7. internal 8. normal 9. random 10. react

LESSON 14

Page 58: 1. indifference 2. demonstration 3. tolerance
4. participation 5. individual 6. resolution 7. voluntary
8. input 9. reform 10. bias **Page 59: A.** 1. individual 2. bias

3. demonstration 4. reform 5. indifference 6. tolerance
7. participation **B.** 1. data 2. plan 3. gift **Page 60:**
A. 1. group 2. retain 3. unacceptance 4. interest 5. forced
6. output **B.** 1.–3. Sentences will vary. 1. resolve
2. participate 3. demonstrate **C.** Sentences will vary.
Page 61: 1. voluntary 2. biased 3. input 4. individual
5. reform 6. resolution 7. indifference 8. tolerance
9. demonstration 10. participation

LESSON 15

Page 62: 1. explanation 2. positive 3. alter 4. engaged
5. indicated 6. probe 7. assured 8. conferred 9. obvious
10. confirmed **Page 63: A.** 1. obvious 2. engage 3. assure
4. positive 5. probe 6. confer **B.** 1. appointment 2. arrow
3. account 4. belief **Page 64: A.** 1.–3. Sentences will vary.
1. disengage 2. reassure 3. reconfirm **B.** 1. a 2. b 3. c 4. b
C. 1. positive 2. obvious 3. probe **Page 65: Across:**
1. engage 5. alter 8. indicate 9. positive 10. probe **Down:**
2. assure 3. explanation 4. confer 6. confirm 7. obvious

LESSON 16

Page 66: 1. contact 2. inherit 3. equip 4. resisted
5. collapsed 6. occupy 7. dedicate 8. unify 9. emerge
10. insert **Page 67: A.** 1. e 2. g 3. b 4. c 5. f 6. a 7. d 8. h
B. 1. friend 2. money **Page 68: A.** 1. noun 2. verb 3. verb
4. noun **B.** 1. opposed 2. addressed 3. attracted notice
4. fill **C.** 1.–4. Sentences will vary. **Page 69:** 1. resist
2. occupy 3. emerge 4. equip 5. dedicate 6. collapse
7. inherit 8. unify 9. contact 10. insert

LESSON 17

Page 70: 1. identical 2. indirect 3. definite 4. legendary
4. authentic 6. secure 7. dramatic 8. fundamental
9. remarkable 10. general **Page 71: A.** 1. synonym—
theatrical; antonym—bland 2. synonym—safe; antonym—
threatened 3. synonym—precise; antonym—vague
4. synonym—same; antonym—dissimilar 5. synonym—
slanted; antonym—straight 6. synonym—elementary;
antonym—unnecessary 7. synonym—extraordinary;
antonym—uninteresting **B.** 1. star 2. typical 3. original
Page 72: A. 1.–3. Sentences will vary. 1. security
2. authenticity 3. definition **B.** 1. c 2. a 3. b 4. c 5. b 6. a 7. c
Page 73: 1. authentic 2. general 3. fundamental 4. identical
5. definite 6. indirect 7. dramatic 8. secure 9. remarkable
10. legendary

LESSON 18

Page 74: 1. proposal 2. influence 3. phase 4. ideals
5. authority 6. scope 7. output 8. structure 9. target
10. development **Page 75: A.** 1. suggestion, plan 2. stage,
step 3. breadth, extent 4. impression, effect 5. goal,
intention 6. power, jurisdiction 7. standard, model
8. evolution, outcome **B.** 1. product 2. tower **Page 76:**
A. 1. information 2. microscope **B.** 1. verb 2. noun 3. verb
4. noun 5. verb 6. noun 7. verb 8. noun 9. noun
10. adjective **C.** 1. develop 2. author 3. propose **Page 77:**
Answers will vary.